Young Vic

BULL
MIKE BARTLETT

This production was originally produced by Sheffield Theatres
and opened at the Young Vic on 8 January 2015

supporting wall

BULL
MIKE BARTLETT

A Supporting Wall / Young Vic co-production

Tony	Adam James
Isobel	Eleanor Matsuura
Carter	Neil Stuke
Thomas	Sam Troughton
Direction	Clare Lizzimore
Design	Soutra Gilmour
Light	Peter Mumford
Sound	Christopher Shutt
Casting	Amy Ball and Lotte Hines
Associate Director	Jonathan O'Boyle
Associate Designer	Rachel Wingate
Associate Lighting Designer	Kati Hind
Production Manager	Marius Ronning
Assistant Production Manager and Stage Manager	Heather Doole
Deputy Stage Manager	Susan Ellicott
Lighting Operator	Sebastian Barresi

Supporting Wall would like to thank Daniel Evans, Peter Tear, Daniel Ryan, Adrian Lukis, Sian Brooke, Emma Brunjes, Claudie Blakley, Nicholas Gleaves, Robin Soans, Nigel Lindsay, Tobias Menzies, Mark Holgate, Sarah Nicholson, Dan Bates, Dan Franklin, Neil McPherson, Sarah Gentle, Mary Hely, Rachel Tackley, Anthony Pins, Thelma Holt, Malcolm Taylor, Kenny Nunez. Special thanks to Alan Buttar at Muse Design.

Bull is supported by Arts Council England through Grants for the Arts, the Unity Theatre Trust, the Ronald Duncan Literary Foundation, the Golsoncott Foundation, the Royal Victoria Hall Foundation, David Tyler and English Touring Theatre's Forge Scheme.

Biographies

MIKE BARTLETT
Theatre includes: *King Charles III* (Almeida/Wyndham's); *An Intervention* (Paines Plough/Watford Palace Theatre); *Medea* (Headlong/Citizens, Glasgow/Watford Palace Theatre); *Chariots of Fire* (Hampstead/Gielgud); *Love, Love, Love* (Paines Plough/Theatre Royal Plymouth/Royal Court); *13* (National Theatre); *Decade* (Headlong); *Earthquakes in London* (Headlong/National Theatre); *Cock* (Royal Court/Duke Theatre, New York); *Contractions, My Child* (Royal Court) and *Artefacts* (Nabokov/Bush/59E59 Theatre, New York).

He has previously been Writer-in-Residence at the Royal Court, National Theatre and Paines Plough.

Film includes: *Earthquakes in London* (in development).

Television includes: *Doctor Foster* and *The Town*.

Radio includes: *The Right Honourable, The Core, Heart, Liam, The Steps, Love Contract, Not Talking* and *The Family Man*.

Awards include: 2011 UK Theatre Awards Best New Play for *Love, Love Love*, and 2010 Olivier Awards for Outstanding Achievement in an Affiliate Theatre for *Cock*, Imison and Tinniswood Awards for *Not Talking* and the Old Vic New Voices Award for *Artefacts*.

CLARE LIZZIMORE – Direction
Theatre includes: *One Day When We Were Young* (Paines Plough/Sheffield Theatres/Shoreditch Town Hall); *Lay Down Your Cross, On the Rocks* (Hampstead); *Pieces of Vincent* (Arcola); *Faces in the Crowd, The Mother* (Royal Court); *Jonah and Otto* (Royal Exchange, Manchester); *Tom Fool* (Citizens, Glasgow/Bush) and *The Most Humane Way to Kill a Lobster* (Theatre503).

As Writer: *Mint* (Royal Court).

Radio includes: *Missing in Action.*

Awards include: Channel 4 Theatre Directors Award and the Arts Foundation Theatre Directing Fellowship. Clare has been resident director at Citizens Theatre, Glasgow and a staff director at the National Theatre.

SOUTRA GILMOUR – Design
Previous Young Vic: *When the World was Green.*

Theatre includes: *The Crucible, The Duchess of Malfi* (Old Vic); *Urinetown* (St James/Apollo); *The Commitments* (Palace); *From Here to Eternity* (Shaftesbury); *Candide* (RSC); *The Ruling Class, Richard III, Macbeth, The Hothouse, The Pride* (Trafalgar Transformed); *From Morning to Midnight, Strange Interlude, Moon on a Rainbow Shawl, Antigone, Double Feature, Shadow of A Boy* (National Theatre); *Assassins, Torchsong Trilogy, Merrily We Roll Along* (Menier Chocolate Factory/Harold Pinter); *A Taste of Honey* (Sheffield Theatres); *Cyrano de Bergerac* (Roundabout Theatre); *Reasons To Be Pretty* (Almeida); *The Night Alive* (Broadway); *Inadmissible Evidence, Piaf, Polar Bears* (Donmar Warehouse); *Into the Woods* (Regents Park/Public Theatre, New York); *In a Forest Dark and Deep* (Vaudeville); *The Little Dog Laughed* (Garrick Theatre); *Three Days of Rain* (Apollo); *The Pride* (Royal Court); *The Tragedy of Thomas Hobbes* (RSC at Wilton's Music Hall); *The Lover/The Collection* (Comedy); *Who's Afraid of Virginia Woolf, Close the Coalhouse Door, Our Friends in the North, Ruby Moon, Son of Man* (Northern Stage); *Last Easter* (Birmingham Repertory Theatre); *Angels in America* (Lyric

Hammersmith); *Bad Jazz, A Brief History of Helen of Troy* (ATC); *The Birthday Party* (Sheffield Crucible); *The Caretaker* (Sheffield Theatres/Tricycle); *Petrol Jesus Nightmare #5* (Traverse, Kosovo) and *Lovers & War* (Stockholm).

Opera includes: *Quartett, Un Ballo in Maschera* (Royal Opera House/Theatre Dortmund); *Opera Shorts 2010/2011, Down By the Greenwood Side, Into the Little Hill* (Royal Opera House); *Anna Bolena, Don Giovanni, Così Fan Tutte, Mary Stuart* (English Touring Opera); *The Shops* (Bregenz Festival); *The Birds, Trouble in Tahiti* (The Opera Group); *El Cimmamon* (Queen Elizabeth Hall); *Saul, Hansel & Gretel, Carmen* (Opera North); *A Better Place* (ENO) and *Girl of Sand* (Almeida).

Awards include: 2012 Evening Standard Award for Best Set Design for *Inadmissible Evidence* and *Antigone.*

PETER MUMFORD – Light

Theatre includes: *Women on the Verge of a Nervous Breakdown* (Playhouse); *Donkey Heart* (Old Red Lion); *Ghosts* (Almeida/Trafalgar Studios); *Stephen Ward, Top Hat* (Aldwych); *Old Times, Absent Friends* (Harold Pinter); *Jumpy* (Royal Court/Duke of York's); *Much Ado About Nothing* (Wyndham's); *The Lion in Winter* (Theatre Royal Haymarket); *An Ideal Husband* (Vaudeville); *A View From the Bridge* (Duke of York); *King Kong* (Global Creatures, Australia); *Scenes from an Execution, Twelfth Night,* (National Theatre); *The Wolf from the Door, Circle Mirror Transformation, In the Republic of Happiness, Our Private Life, Sucker Punch* (Royal Court); *Love and Information* (Royal Court/New York Theatre); *Cock* (Royal Court/Duke on 42nd Street, New York); *Other Desert Cities, Richard II* (Old Vic); *Wonderland, The Last of the Duchess* (Hampstead); *The Dark Earth and the Light* Sky (Almeida); *King Lear* (Chichester Festival Theatre/BAM, New York); *The Same Deep Water as Me* (Donmar Warehouse); *A Taste of Honey, Betrayal* (Sheffield Theatres); *Testament* (Dublin Theatre Festival); *The BFG* (Birmingham Repertory Theatre) and *Accolade* (St James).

Opera and Dance includes: *La Traviata* (Glyndebourne); *Werther, Faust, Carmen, Peter Grimes, 125th Anniversary* Gala (Met Opera House, New York); *Manon Lescaut* (Baden Baden); *The Soldier's Tale, Pierrot* (Chicago Symphony Orchestra); *Passion* (Minnesota Opera); *The Damnation of Faust, Lucrezia Borgia, Bluebeard's Castle* (ENO); *Petrushka* (Scottish Ballet); *Faster, Take Five* (Birmingham Royal Ballet); *Il Trovatore* (Opera National De Paris); *Fidelio, Two Widows, Don Giovanni, The Ring* (Scottish Opera); *Midsummer Marriage* (Chicago Lyric Opera); *Eugene Onegin* and *The Bartered Bride* (Royal Opera House).

Awards include: Olivier Award for Outstanding Achievement in Dance for *The Glass Blew* and *Fearful Symmetries,* Olivier Award for Best Lighting for *The Bacchai,* Knight of Illumination Award for *Sucker Punch* and the Helpmann and Green Room Awards for *King Kong.*

CHRISTOPHER SHUTT – Sound

Christopher Shutt was previously Head of Sound at the Royal Court and the National Theatre.

Theatre includes: *The James Plays, War Horse, The Effect, Coram Boy, Every Good Boy Deserves Favour* (National Theatre); *A Disappearing Number, Mnemonic* (Complicite); *Love and Information* (Royal Court); *Privacy* and *Piaf* (Donmar Warehouse).

Awards include: 2011 Tony Award for Best Sound Design for *War Horse* and the New York Drama Desk Award for *War Horse, Mnemonic* and *Not About Nightingales.*

JONATHAN O'BOYLE – Associate Director
Previous Young Vic: *All the Ways to Say Goodbye* (Young Vic 5 Plays) and *The Scottsboro Boys.*
Theatre includes: *Made in Britain* (Old Red Lion); *This Is My Family* (Sheffield Lyceum/UK tour); *Bash: Latterday Plays* (Trafalgar Studios/Old Red Lion); *Water Under the Board* (Theatre503); *Last Online Today, Guinea Pigs* (Sheffield Crucible); *The Good, The Bad and the Broken Hearted* (Ronnie Scott's) and *The Monster Bride* (Tristan Bates).
As Assistant Director: *Amadeus* (Chichester Festival Theatre); *Manon* (Royal Opera House); *My Fair Lady, The Village Bike* and *This Is My Family* (Sheffield Theatres).

ADAM JAMES – Tony
Theatre includes: *King Charles III* (Almeida/Wyndham's); *Rapture, Blister, Burn, Tiger Country* (Hampstead); *13, Blood and Gifts, Gethsemane* (National Theatre); *Much Ado About Nothing* (Wyndham's); *Now or Later, My Child* (Royal Court); *The Pride* (MCC Theatre, New York); *Rabbit* (Old Red Lion/ Trafalgar Studios/59E59 Theatres, New York); *Original Sin* (Sheffield Crucible); *The Glass Menagerie* (Minerva); *Time and the Conways, Snake in Fridge, King Lear* and *Poor Superman* (Royal Exchange, Manchester).
Film includes: *A Little Chaos, Kilimanjaro, Last Chance Harvey, Mother of Tears, Road to Guantanamo* and *De-Lovely.*
Television includes: *Coalition, Grantchester, The Assets, The Game, Crimson Field, Churchill: The War Letters, Law & Order, Family Tree, Vexed, Miranda, Law & Order Los Angeles, Lewis, A Touch of Frost, Foyle's War, The Execution of Gary Glitter, Doctor Who, Sleep With Me, Hustle, Consuming Passions, Wired, Secret Diary of a Call Girl, Ashes to Ashes, Extras, The Commander, The Amazing Mrs Pritchard, Waking the Dead, Judge John Deed, Love Soup, England Expects, The Lost Battalion, Murder on the Orient Express, Band of Brothers, Silent Witness* and *Sharpe's Regiment.*

ELEANOR MATSUURA – Isobel
Previous Young Vic: *The Changeling.*
Theatre includes: *Danton's Death* (National Theatre); *Coriolanus* (RSC); *Enron* (Noël Coward) and *24 Hour Plays: Revolution* (Old Vic).
Film includes: *Spooks: The Greater Good, Alan Partridge: Alpha Papa, Love Punch Magicians, Breaking and Entering, After the Rain, Residue* and *Lady in the Van.*
Television includes: *Da Vinci's Demons, Money, Silk, Utopia, Hunter, FM, The Old Guys, Lead Balloon, Doctor Who, Doctors, Casualty, Trial and Retribution, My Family, After You've Gone, 9/11: Dawn to Dusk, Doctors, EastEnders, A Very Social Secretary, Green Wing, Extras, Holby City, Hustle* and *The Fades.*

NEIL STUKE – Carter
Theatre includes: *Six Actors in Search of a Director* (Charing Cross Theatre); *Season's Greetings* (National Theatre); *Rookery Nook* (Menier Chocolate Factory); *Boeing-Boeing* (Comedy); *Bad Jazz* (Theatre Royal Plymouth); *A Night at the Dogs* (Soho); *Blue/Orange* (Duchess); *Entertaining Mr Sloane* (Arts); *Threesome* (Lyric Hammersmith); *The Bullet* (Donmar Warehouse); *Featuring Loretta, The Philanderer* (Hampstead); *Grace Note* (Peter Hall); *Mojo* (Duke of York's); *Clocks and Whistles and Goldhawk Road* (Bush); *Not a Game for Boys* (Royal Court); *Women in Mind* (Watford Palace Theatre/USA tour); *What the Butler Saw, Drinking in America, A View from the Bridge,*

Romeo and Juliet (Royal Exchange); *The Grapes of Wrath* (Sheffield Crucible) and *Frankie and Johnny* (Chichester Festival Theatre).

Film includes: *Out on a Limb, Mother Theresa, School for Seduction, Christy Malry's Own Double Entry, Circus, The Suicide Club, Dead Bolt Dead, Mad Cows, Sliding Doors, If Only, Shark Hunt, Masculine Mesculine, Century* and *Father's Day* (as producer).

Television includes: *The Interceptor, Lewis, Plebs, Silk, One Night, Death in Paradise, New Tricks, Miss Marple, Reggie Perrin, Midsomer Murders, Monday Monday, The Catherine Tate Show, Kingdom, The Bill, Elizabeth: The Virgin Queen, Soundproof, Chopra's Town, 20,000 Streets Under the Sky, Faith, The Hitch, Bedtime, Murphy's Law, Grafters, Murder in Mind, Serious and Organised, Trust, Office Gossip, Sins, At Home with the Braithwaites, Silent Witness, Seesaw, Pie in the Sky, Wing and a Prayer, Game On, A Touch of Frost, Cardiac Arrest, Poirot* and *Resort to Murder.*

SAM TROUGHTON – Thomas
Previous Young Vic: *Three Sisters.*

Theatre includes: *King Lear, Buried Child, The Coast of Utopia* trilogy, *Tartuffe* (National Theatre); *Mint, Death Tax, The President has come to see you, Love, Love, Love* (Royal Court); *A Streetcar Named Desire* (Liverpool Playhouse); *Morte D'Arthur, Romeo and Juliet, The Grain Store, Julius Caesar, The Winter's Tale, Richard III, Henry VI Part III, Henry VI Part II, Henry VI Part I, The Taming of the Shrew* (RSC); *A Midsummer Night's Dream* (RSC/City of London Sinfornia/Cannizaro Park); *An Oak Tree* (Birmingham Repertory Theatre); *As You Like It* (Sheffield Crucible); *Nathan the Wise* (Hampstead); *Hamlet* (Orange Tree); *The Other Shore* (Attic Theatre Company) and *School for Scandal* (Derby Playhouse).

Film includes: *Spirit Trap, Alien vs. Predator, Vera Drake* and *Sylvia.*

Television includes: *The Hollow Crown II: The War of the Roses, Dancing on the Edge, The Town, Holby City, Silent Witness, Robin Hood (Series 1, 2 & 3), Hex II, Messiah III, Gunpowder, Treason and Plot, Judge John Deed, Seven Wonders of the Industrial Age: The Sewer King, Ultimate Force, Blue Dove, Foyle's War* and *Summer in the Suburbs.*

SUPPORTING WALL

Producing company Supporting Wall was founded in 2008 by Ben Monks and Will Young, focusing primarily on new writing in London and on tour.

Previous productions include the world premiere of Philip Ridley's *Dark Vanilla Jungle* (Royal Exchange, Manchester/Pleasance Edinburgh/UK tour/Soho Theatre), winner of the Scotsman Fringe First Award and nominated for the Stage Best Solo Performance Award. The company also premiered Ridley's plays *Tender Napalm* (Southwark Playhouse/UK tour), nominated for an Evening Standard Award, and *Moonfleece* (Riverside Studios/UK tour). Supporting Wall will present Ridley's comedy *Radiant Vermin* at Tobacco Factory Bristol and Soho Theatre in March–April 2015.

Other recent work includes premieres of Timberlake Wertenbaker's *Our Ajax* (Southwark Playhouse); Chris Lee's social-work drama *Shallow Slumber* (Soho Theatre); chamber opera *Yellow* (Tête à Tête Festival) and rapid-response political theatre event *Election Drama* (New Players Theatre), described by the *New Statesman* as 'a breathtaking feat of theatrical chutzpah'.

Supporting Wall was supported by a SOLT/TMA Stage One Bursary, and was nominated for the Off West End Best Producer Award in 2011 and 2012.

www.supportingwall.com

supporting
wall

Young Vic

The Cut Bar & Restaurant

Our bar and restaurant is a relaxing place to meet and eat. An inspired mix of classic and original play-themed dishes made from fresh, free-range and organic ingredients creates an exciting menu.
www.thecutbar.com

Our shows

We present the widest variety of classics, new plays, forgotten works and music theatre. We tour and co-produce extensively within the UK and internationally.

Our artists

Our shows are created by some of the world's great theatre people alongside the most adventurous of the younger generation. This fusion makes the Young Vic one of the most exciting theatres in the world.

Our audience

...is famously the youngest and most diverse in London. We encourage those who don't think theatre is 'for them' to make it part of their lives. We give 10% of our tickets to schools and neighbours irrespective of box office demand, and keep prices low.

Our partners near at hand

Each year we engage with 10,000 local people – individuals and groups of all kinds including schools and colleges – by exploring theatre on and off stage. From time to time we invite our neighbours to appear on our stage alongside professionals.

Our partners further away

By co-producing with leading theatre, opera, and dance companies from London and around the world we create shows neither partner could achieve alone.

The Young Vic is a company limited by guarantee, registered in England No. 1188209.

VAT registration No. 236 673 348

The Young Vic (registered charity number 268876) receives public funding from:

Get more from the Young Vic Online

 youngvictheatre

 @youngvictheatre

 youngviclondon

 youngviclondon.wordpress.com

@youngvictheatre

Sign up to receive email updates at **youngvic.org/register**

GET INVOLVED WITH THE YOUNG VIC

'The best theatre in town' *Telegraph*

'The go-to venue for remixed classics' *Financial Times*

'The sexiest theatre in London' *Time Out*

To produce our sell-out, award-winning shows and provide thousands of free activities through our Taking Part programme requires major investment. Find out how you can make a difference and get involved.

As an individual... become a Friend to jump the queues, a Soul Mate to go behind the scenes or remember the Young Vic in your will.

As a company... take advantage of our flexible memberships, exciting sponsorship opportunities, corporate workshops, CSR engagement and venue hire.

As a trust or foundation... support our innovative and forward-thinking programmes on stage and off.

Are you interested in events... hire a space in our award-winning building and we can work with you to create truly memorable workshops, conferences or parties.

For more information visit

youngvic.org/support us

020 7922 2810

Charity Registration No. 268876

SUPPORTING THE YOUNG VIC

The Young Vic relies on the generous support of many individuals, trusts, foundations, and companies to produce our work, on and off stage. For their recent support we thank

Public Funders
Arts Council England
British Council
Creative & Cultural Skills
Lambeth Borough Council
Southwark Council

Corporate Partners
Barclays
Berkeley Group
Bloomberg
Edelman
Markit
Taylor Wessing LLP
Wahaca

Corporate Members
aka
Bloomberg
Clifford Chance
Ingenious Media PLC
Latham & Watkins
Memery Crystal
Mishcon de Reya
Royal Bank of Scotland
Wisdom Council

Partners
Tony & Gisela Bloom
Patrick Handley
Chris & Jane Lucas
Patrick McKenna
Simon & Midge Palley
Jon & NoraLee Sedmak
Rita & Paul Skinner
Bruno Wang
Anda & Bill Winters

Soul Mates
Ensemble
Royce & Rotha Bell
Beatrice Bondy
Caroline & Ian Cormack
Jill & Justin Manson
Miles Morland
Catherine Schreiber
Dasha Shenkman
Justin Shinebourne
Sir Patrick Stewart

Jane Attias
Chris & Frances Bates
Anthony & Karen Beare
The Bickertons
Katie Bradford
CJ & LM Braithwaite
Sandra Carlisle
Tim & Caroline Clark
Kay Ellen Consolver
Felicia Crystal
Miel de Botton
Lucy & Spencer de Grey
Annabel Duncan-Smith
Robyn Durie

Jennifer & Jeff Eldredge
Don Ellwood &
    Sandra Johnigan
Gillian Frumkin
Paul Gambaccini
Beth & Gary Glynn
Annika Goodwille
Sarah Hall
Caroline Hansberry
Richard Hardman & Family
Madeleine Hodgkin
Nik Holttum &
    Helen Brannigan
Jane Horrocks
Miss Lottie Hughes
Linden Ife
Maxine Isaacs
Suzanne & Michael Johnson
Tom Keatinge
John Kinder & Gerry Downey
Mr & Mrs Herbert Kretzmer
Lady Rayne Lacey
Carol Lake
Jude Law
Ann Lewis
Tony Mackintosh
James & Sue Macmillan
Michael McCabe
Karen McHugh
Ian McKellen
Juliet Medforth
Barbara Minto
Joseph Morgan
Ann & Gavin Neath CBE
Georgia Oetker
Sally O'Neill
Rob & Lesley O'Rahilly
Powerscourt
André Ptaszynski
Barbara Reeves
Anthony & Sally Salz
Charles & Donna Scott
Sarah Selkirk
Bhagat Sharma
Lois Sieff
Nicola Stanhope
Karen Taylor
Jan & Michael Topham
Totally Theatre Productions
The Ulrich Family
The Ury Trust
Marina Vaizey
Donna & Richard Vinter
Jimmy & Carol Walker
Rob Wallace
Edgar & Judith Wallner
George & Patricia White

Trust Supporters
95.8 Capital FM's Help a
    Capital Child
Andor Charitable Trust
Austin & Hope Pilkington Trust
BBC Children in Need
Backstage Trust
Boris Karloff Foundation
Boshier Hinton Foundation
The City Bridge Trust
Clifford Chance Foundation
Clore Duffield Foundation
John S Cohen Foundation
The Co-operative Membership
    Community Fund
David Laing Foundation
The Dr. Mortimer and Theresa
    Sackler Foundation
D'Oyly Carte Charitable Trust
Embassy of the Kingdom of the
    Netherlands
Equitable Charitable Trust
The Eranda Foundation
Ernest Cook Trust
The Foyle Foundation
Garfield Weston Foundation
Garrick Charitable Trust
Genesis Foundation
Golden Bottle Trust
Golsoncott Foundation
H&M Foundation
Jerwood Charitable Foundation
Joanies Fund
John Ellerman Foundation
John Thaw Foundation
J. Paul Getty Jnr. Charitable
    Trust
The Limbourne Trust
The Mackintosh Foundation
Martin Bowley Charitable Trust
Mrs Margaret Guido's
    Charitable Trust
Newcomen Collett Foundation
The Noel Coward Foundation
The Nomura Charitable Trust
The Portrack Charitable Trust
The Red Hill Trust
Richard Radcliffe Charitable
    Trust
The Richenthal Foundation
Royal Norwegian Embassy
The Sackler Trust
Sir Walter St John's
    Educational Charity
The Wolfson Foundation

*and all other donors who wish
to remain anonymous.*

markit®

Proud to be the lead sponsor of the

Young Vic's Funded Ticket Programme

Enabling theatre to be enjoyed by all

Young Vic

Theatre

markit.com

BULL

Mike Bartlett

Bull was first performed at the Crucible Studio Theatre, Sheffield, on 6 February 2013. The cast was as follows:

TONY	Adam James
CARTER	Adrian Lukis
ISOBEL	Eleanor Matsuura
THOMAS	Sam Troughton

Director	Clare Lizzimore
Designer	Soutra Gilmour
Lighting Designer	Peter Mumford
Sound Designer	Christopher Shutt

Bull transferred to 59E59 Theaters, New York, as part of the Brits Off Broadway season on 25 April 2013, with the following change to the cast:

CARTER	Neil Stuke

Acknowledgements

Thanks to: Daniel Bates, Daniel Evans, Soutra Gilmour, Neil McPherson, and particularly, Clare Lizzimore.

M.B.

Characters

THOMAS
ISOBEL
TONY
CARTER

The audience is raked down towards the actors.
There should be a minimum of scenery, props and furniture, in
order to keep the focus on the drama of the scene.

(/) means the next speech begins at that point.
(–) means the next line interrupts.
(...) at the end of a speech means it trails off. On its own it
indicates a pressure, expectation or desire to speak.

A line with no full stop at the end indicates that the next speech
follows on immediately.

A speech with no written dialogue indicates a character
deliberately remaining silent.

Blank space between speeches in the dialogue indicates a
silence equal to the length of the space.

This text went to press before the end of rehearsals and so may
differ slightly from the play as performed.

ISOBEL   You've got…

THOMAS   What?

ISOBEL   You've got something just…

THOMAS   What?

ISOBEL   No the other side.

THOMAS   There?

ISOBEL   Yes. No it's still there.

THOMAS   Gone? Has it gone now?

ISOBEL   Well…

THOMAS   Where is he?

ISOBEL   He's coming. Look at you.

THOMAS   What? What are you talking about?

ISOBEL   Step left step right –

THOMAS   Stop it.

ISOBEL   – dancing all over the room. Calm down.

THOMAS   I am calm. I'm standing perfectly still.

ISOBEL   You are now. But before you were like oo
            oo oo.

THOMAS   Stop criticising me.

            I'm very cool about all this.

ISOBEL   You're not cool about anything.

THOMAS   It's just one of those days, one of those
            meetings you know, there's no reason to be
            particularly fussed about it.

ISOBEL	now you're fussed
THOMAS	I mean he's just a man, isn't he?
ISOBEL	I believe so.
THOMAS	With a job to do.
ISOBEL	Did you wear that deliberately?
THOMAS	Did I wear what deliberately?
ISOBEL	Your suit.
THOMAS	Yes I wore my suit deliberately yes, I didn't accidentally wear it, what would that even mean –
ISOBEL	It means your suit looks cheap.
THOMAS	Yeah. Well. I didn't wear it for you.
ISOBEL	No I think you wore it because you think it's your best one, but actually I think the other one, the one you wear every day, I think that's better.
THOMAS	You really are a bitch.
ISOBEL	Hey. Hey. I'm just saying, since we're waiting, since we're making conversation best as we can, I'm simply saying your suit isn't as *great* as you think it is. That's allowed. Expressing my opinion. Your suit, whether you like it or not, is a talking point. I'm not being *a bitch*. You should be grateful I was making conversation at all.
THOMAS	You've never liked me.
ISOBEL	Where the fuck is this coming from?
TONY	Are we ready?

THOMAS	We look ready don't we? Stupid fucking question.
TONY	Is he going to wear that suit?
THOMAS	For fuck's –
ISOBEL	Yes he is.
THOMAS	TALK TO ME! I'm here. Look.
TONY	Why isn't he wearing his best one?
ISOBEL	This is what I was / saying.
THOMAS	This is my best one.
TONY	Oh right. Really?
ISOBEL	Look you see you have to accept it now, I'm not messing with you, your suit will count against you. And Tony agrees so –
THOMAS	Alright, I won't make an effort next time.
ISOBEL	I don't think there'll be a next time. Not for you. I mean from my point of view your suit is good news. Your suit is exactly what I want to see you wearing. Means I'm one up before we've even begun. I was just trying to be nice.
THOMAS	He should be here. Have you heard anything from him?
TONY	What?
THOMAS	We're in the same room. You heard what I said. So why did you just say what?
TONY	What?
THOMAS	I said had you heard anything and instead of replying you said what? So it wasn't that you didn't hear me, it's implying a contempt for my question.

TONY	What?
THOMAS	I could hit you sometimes.
TONY	Why would he call me?
THOMAS	You're the team leader. Officially anyway.
TONY	Officially oo owch I'm offended. No. He knows the time we're meeting so why would he call? He's always on time. He knows we'll be here, I don't understand your question. Hence my reply: 'What?'
ISOBEL	It's still there.
THOMAS	What?
ISOBEL	The thing. Just…
THOMAS	Where? I thought you said it was –
ISOBEL	Yeah but it kind of –
THOMAS	Have you got a mirror?
ISOBEL	Sorry.
THOMAS	Yeah if I looked like you I wouldn't bother either.
ISOBEL	A compliment. Thank you.
THOMAS	I meant –
ISOBEL	I know what you meant.
	There's a mirror in the bathroom.
	Thomas?
	You know where the bathroom is?
THOMAS	Yeah but I don't want to leave do I? In case he gets here when I'm gone. So.

ISOBEL	Okay Fine.
	Fine.
	…but I really think you should have a look. Right?
TONY	Yeah.
ISOBEL	I mean it's… it's really… isn't it?
TONY	Yeah mate, mate's favour, it's really…
THOMAS	Okay. I see. You're fucking with me.
ISOBEL	On your head be it. Literally.
THOMAS	You really are not sexy I want to say that. You should know that.
ISOBEL	Thank you Thomas, but your opinion is one of the least important.
THOMAS	So fucking icy. I could take you to a country hotel and put you in front of the fire, leave you all night, and I guarantee you'd still be as fucking frozen as you are right now. Icy, hard. Tight.
TONY	Tight. Isobel. He said tight.
ISOBEL	I know, what a weird thing to say, what do you mean tight?
THOMAS	Tight. Anal. You're sucked up. It's like you're keeping everything in. Tight. Tight. Tight.
ISOBEL	Go on.
THOMAS	I mean that in the unlikely event of anyone trying to fuck you Isobel they'd knock and

they'd knock but there's no one at home is
there? Not in that department. I have a feeling
the door has been shut so long, you don't
know if it opens. Probably don't even know
where the door is.

ISOBEL   Jesus Tony what can he mean? I think it's a
            metaphor of *some kind* / but...

TONY   You know that thing about the suit?

THOMAS   Yes.

TONY   I was messing with you.

THOMAS   Right.

TONY   I was standing outside, I heard your
            conversation. Heard what you were talking
            about.

THOMAS   Okay.

TONY   Thought it would be funny to join in.

THOMAS   Okay.

            So the suit – ?

TONY   The suit's fine.

THOMAS   Okay.

            And have I got something on my head?

TONY   Yeah. That's true, you have. It's just, on the
            right.
            No. The right.
            No. Sorry mate.
            It's still...
            It's quite distracting.
            Where were you born?

THOMAS   What?

TONY	You heard me. Or was that contempt?
THOMAS	Contempt.
TONY	So?
THOMAS	Why do you want to know?
TONY	Why are you so cagey?
THOMAS	I'm not cagey, I'm careful, I'm careful with you because of what you do all the time.
TONY	What we do all the time I have no idea what you're talking about I'm just making conversation here just asking a really simple question basic kind of simple kind of thing you say and yet and yet still no sign of an answer from you.
THOMAS	
TONY	Is there? Still no… sign… just standing there looking like a startled sheep.
THOMAS	Ringwood
TONY	I'm sorry?
THOMAS	Where I was born.
TONY	Ringwood.
THOMAS	Yeah.
TONY	That's in the New Forest yes?
THOMAS	Why?
TONY	Why is it in the New Forest, don't know.
THOMAS	Why did you ask where I'm born?
TONY	What did your father do?
THOMAS	Why are you suddenly asking me these questions, you're such a couple of shits.
ISOBEL	I haven't spoken in what, a minute?

TONY	What did he do?
	Your dad?

THOMAS	I'm not saying.
TONY	Is it embarrassing or something?
THOMAS	I'm keeping my life to myself why would I tell you two? You'd use it against me.
TONY	Against you? Thomas. Come on. What is this? Jesus. We're just making conversation. We're just talking. That's a nice thing for us to do.
ISOBEL	This is what I was saying.
TONY	You take everything so seriously. Fuck.
	I mean we could all sit in silence if you'd rather.

THOMAS	He was a maths teacher.
TONY	A maths teacher?

THOMAS	What?
TONY	Funny.

THOMAS	What did yours do?
TONY	He's a surgeon.
THOMAS	What? He still is?

TONY   Still is. Yep. Still got hands, steady as a rock.
              Silver fox I think he is these days, nurses they
              love him, he tells me these stories when we're
              in the pub or out walking, he's still very fit,
              very youthful, tells me these stories when we
              go, play golf together. But yours, you said he
              was a maths teacher – was – so he must be…
              older. Than mine. You said he's not a maths
              teacher any more, so you mean he's now…
              what? Retired?

THOMAS   Dead.

TONY   Oh.
              Oh. I'm sorry to hear that.

THOMAS   I really don't want to talk about this?

TONY   What did he die of?

              Was it maths?

              Cos I hate maths.

THOMAS   What did your dad do?

ISOBEL

THOMAS

ISOBEL   …

THOMAS   ?

ISOBEL   Me.

THOMAS   What?

ISOBEL   He did me. He abused me.

THOMAS

ISOBEL

THOMAS   I don't believe a fucking word you say.

ISOBEL	Oh how sympathetic. Thank you Thomas tell you this thing this secret that's actually quite personal actually? And you're just –
THOMAS	If it was true you wouldn't just come out and say it like that, like 'I was abused' you'd be more…
ISOBEL	More?
THOMAS	…
ISOBEL	You want me to be ashamed of it, you're telling me how to behave?
THOMAS	You're a lying cow / this is –
ISOBEL	You want me to hide it?
THOMAS	Do you know if that's true?
TONY	What?
THOMAS	That.
TONY	Yeah I know if it's true.
THOMAS	And?
TONY	You're being quite insensitive.
	Her father used to come into her room when she was a child and do things to her, she'll tell you the details if you want, but trust me you don't. She told me all about it. When she did, when she told me, it made my eyes water. Not with tears. With pain Thomas, with excruciating hurt.
THOMAS	Well… alright. If it's true, then I'm really so very very sorry to hear it, it must've been *awful* Isobel, the flowers are on their way, believe me, but even if it isn't complete crap I

can't think why you would bring it up now
other than to *use* it.

ISOBEL   *Use* it?

THOMAS   Yeah.

ISOBEL   I'm sorry I'm going to have to leave in a
               minute.

THOMAS   Yeah yeah. Alright.
               I believe you.
               Okay?

               Whatever you want.

ISOBEL   Maybe now you can see why your tight
               comment earlier was a bit offensive? If I am
               tight, maybe there's a reason.

THOMAS   It's no excuse for being a bitch now.

ISOBEL   You always call me a bitch, you never say
               anything about him.

TONY   My dad isn't a surgeon Thomas. He's a
               taxman. Not youthful at all. He sits in a chair
               most of the time. We hardly speak.

ISOBEL   See?
               See?
               He's always playing with you and you never
               stand up to him. Be a man, have some fucking
               balls, then someone might find you attractive.
               Thomas.
               You might suddenly become a bit just even a
               bit, impressive.
               They might keep you on.

THOMAS   I don't need advice.

ISOBEL   Stop staring at the floor, stop shuffling around
               like an autistic penguin. Don't pick your
               teeth. Don't hunch. Stand up to him, stand up

                straight, smile a bit, you never know, you
                might win.

                I mean you won't.

                But you might.

THOMAS   What did I do? There must've been a day,
                ages ago, when I did something to you two.
                That pissed you off.

ISOBEL   No.

THOMAS   And after that you decided to make my life –

TONY   This again. Look mate, Thomas, mate, me
                and her, we're both very normal people,
                honestly this isn't a thing against you, you
                have to understand that, you seem to have it
                in your head that we're always attacking
                you, and we're not. We're really not.
                Promise.
                Really.
                Promise.

ISOBEL   It's paranoia.

THOMAS   Paranoia.

ISOBEL   Do you have history of mental illness in your
                family?

THOMAS   Actually…

ISOBEL   Yes?

THOMAS   My mother died of Alzheimer's.

ISOBEL   That's a bit sick.

THOMAS   What?

ISOBEL   Making that up.

THOMAS   And making up some abuse story isn't?

ISOBEL   I wasn't.
              Making. It up.

              But this Alzheimer's thing –

THOMAS   What?

ISOBEL   Come on.

THOMAS

ISOBEL

THOMAS   How did you know?

ISOBEL   You twitch. Your right eyebrow.

              It gets worse when you lie. Like Pinocchio's
              nose. But weirder.

TONY   Apparently with the last lot that had to do
              this, they had a few drinks, he asked them
              questions, they had a few more, he kept
              asking, you see he's old-fashioned in that
              way, respects people who can hold their
              drink, who can mix business with pleasure
              cos as he sees it that's where the real work is
              done, so it's the way he likes to choose. He
              calls it doing his weeding.

THOMAS   Really.

TONY   Oh but you don't drink do you?

THOMAS   As if you forgot.

TONY   I'm sure he won't mind if you don't take
              part.

THOMAS   Of course he'll mind. If that's the assessment.
            If that's how he decides. Of course he'll –

ISOBEL   Would you drink if that was how he chose? If
            that was actually how it was done, would you
            sacrifice your morals for staying on here?

THOMAS   Yeah of course it's not –

ISOBEL   So this whole not drinking thing, this is –

THOMAS   I've never drunk I prefer it that way. But it's
            not a thing, if I had to –

TONY   Yeah but if you've never drunk, and then you
            did, even one, you'd be out and under in
            seconds it would be a mess, Thomas, nah you
            would do much better to say sorry sir I don't
            drink.

THOMAS   Why do you hate me?

ISOBEL   Do you have a girlfriend?

THOMAS   I've just realised…

ISOBEL   You don't / right?

THOMAS   All the stuff I thought I knew you could've
            made it all up couldn't you?

TONY   Could've done / yeah.

THOMAS   So like I think you live in a top-floor flat, in
            the centre of town, and in the basement car
            park you keep a Porsche that was a present
            from your uncle, and your girlfriend is called
            Cindy who lives in Paris and works as a
            model, and you trained as an architect, you're
            a world-class poker player, part-time fireman,
            and five years ago you got your pilot's
            licence. But now I'm saying it out loud all
            that it sounds…

TONY	Unconvincing?
ISOBEL	You're very strangely proportioned Thomas, I mean physically.
THOMAS	And you. You as well. You could be anyone.
ISOBEL	I asked you a question.
	Thomas.
THOMAS	What?
ISOBEL	Girlfriend?
THOMAS	Why? Are you offering?
ISOBEL	Ha ha ha ha ha ha. Ha.
	No. I wasn't.
THOMAS	Do you know something?
ISOBEL	Something? What?
THOMAS	You look like you –
ISOBEL	If I knew something why would I ask?
THOMAS	No. I don't have a girlfriend.
ISOBEL	No I can't imagine the sort of girl who'd –
TONY	Have you printed out your sales figures?
THOMAS	I…
	No.
TONY	Okay.
THOMAS	What?
TONY	Nothing.
THOMAS	Have you?
TONY	Of course.

THOMAS	You think he'll want the sales figures?
TONY	Possible isn't it, given the nature of the meeting?
ISOBEL	Likely I'd say.
THOMAS	You as well?
ISOBEL	Absolutely. Why? What have you done?
THOMAS	I thought this was just a preliminary chat.
ISOBEL	Did you?
TONY	Did you?
	Look… Thomas.
	We've both not only printed out our individual and collective sales figures, but we've completed a report on this first six months. We've put all of that together and ringbound it, with a pearlescent card cover in electric blue. Like this.
ISOBEL	See?
TONY	Haven't you?
THOMAS	When did you decide on this?
TONY	Tuesday, I think we… yes, spoke about it…
THOMAS	Not the fucking figures, the idea that if you work together you two will be through and I'll be the one who'll go.
TONY	You think there's a plan? That we sat down, Isobel and me at some point and said if we really undermine this little one, this one who has strangely shaped shoulders, if we just dent his confidence all the time, then he'll fuck up and we'll go through.

THOMAS   Exactly.

ISOBEL   You think we get on? Him and me? I hate him
                even more than you.
                I mean yes, you're like any physically odd
                man, talking too much, strange gestures,
                yapping away, does get annoying, but
                essentially you're harmless. He on the other
                hand is a predator. He's hard and fast. He's
                incredibly selfish. He runs marathons so he
                can sleep with the charity workers. He is in
                fact desperate to sleep with me, which I don't
                want to do, not that I wouldn't, I mean if you
                look at his torso, he's built like a shithouse,
                we should do that actually show him your
                torso in a minute…

TONY   Fine.

ISOBEL   But unfortunately for me, and Tony, I can't
                sleep with him because of my problem that
                we discussed earlier. But he did sleep with
                my friend Julie – took her for a ride in both
                senses, told her all this stuff he said he felt,
                then left her, she was very upset, thought
                she'd found Mr Right. That same month he
                went behind my back on the Stratton deal,
                you remember that one I had, he went
                straight behind my back and clinched it. I
                mean he's a real threat. And you should hear
                how he treats me when you're not there.
                When you're not there him and me, we're
                like a bear and a lion. I wouldn't trust him
                as far as I can throw him and I can't throw
                him that's obvious. We don't get on at all.

                Go on then. Show him your torso.

TONY   Right.

THOMAS	What are you doing? Fuck's sake. What if Carter comes in?
TONY	He won't. He called earlier and said he was running twenty minutes late.
THOMAS	You said he hadn't called.
TONY	I asked you why he would. I didn't say he hadn't.
THOMAS	
TONY	Stand up then.
THOMAS	I don't want to see your fucking *torso*.
TONY	Come on, up up up. Uppy uppy uppy. Isobel help him
THOMAS	Don't fucking touch me.
ISOBEL	Ooh.
TONY	Stand up or we'll be nasty to you.
THOMAS	You are being nasty.
TONY	Really nasty.
THOMAS	…
TONY	Now.
ISOBEL	See what I mean. Shithouse. Should be his name. Tony Shithouse. Look. Not an inch of goodness. Sheer muscular wanker. Not like you, flabby little thing aren't you? Lots of goodness in you. But this one. Different kettle of fish. He's boiled down. He's a piranha.

TONY	Touch it.
THOMAS	I'm not doing this. Put it down.
TONY	Touch it! Go on.
THOMAS	If I touch it you'll both sit down?
TONY	Promise.
	Now put your whole hand on it.
THOMAS	You said.
TONY	I lied.
THOMAS	…
TONY	Okay okay, this time, if you put your whole hand on it, we'll really sit down. Leave you alone. Really. Won't we?
ISOBEL	Yeah.
TONY	Now your face.
THOMAS	Okay, fuck you, we're not at school.
ISOBEL	I will.
THOMAS	I've got other things to think about right now. Today might not matter to you but I'm –
TONY	Come on Thomas this is just fun, it's what we're saying lighten up.
ISOBEL	If I do it, will you do it afterwards?
THOMAS	And then we'll all sit down?
ISOBEL	Yeah.

THOMAS   Fine.

ISOBEL   Mmmmmmmmm.

                Go on then. Your turn.

THOMAS   No. Actually no, I don't have to do this.

ISOBEL   You made me a deal.

THOMAS   It doesn't mean anything. Put your face
                against his chest what the fuck is that. What
                the fuck is put your face against his chest Oh I
                know let's play that game, put your face
                against his chest. No. No. I've had enough.

ISOBEL   He said he'd do it.

TONY   I know.

ISOBEL   And now you're what? Going back on it.

THOMAS   Yeah I'm going back on it. I'm really sorry. I
                apologise *profusely*.

TONY   She said if she did it, you'd do it that was the
                deal.

THOMAS   I'm backing out of the deal.

TONY   You can't.

THOMAS   I have.

TONY   You can't.

THOMAS   So come on that's – we've only got five
                minutes now before he comes what else is
                there you haven't told me, is there anything

else apart from the fact he's running late is
there any other bits of information you're
supposed to –

TONY   Er... Thomas. We're talking to you. We've
              still got an issue to resolve.

THOMAS   ...

TONY   As your team leader, I don't like my colleagues
              playing stupid buggers with each other making
              promises they don't keep. So come over here
              and put your face against my chest.

THOMAS   Don't start using all that, you know I don't
              give a shit about any of that team-leader stuff.
              You have no authority over me. In a minute
              Carter is going to come in here and pick two
              of us to carry on. Send one of us out. Are you
              really going to explain to him what the
              problem is? Do you want to say Mr Carter,
              Isobel put her face against my chest on the
              understanding that Thomas would do the
              same and now he won't. You say that, you'll
              sound about five years old. Won't you?

ISOBEL   I'm really surprised.

TONY   I know.

ISOBEL   We were just having fun.

TONY   He doesn't get it.

ISOBEL   You seem to be one of those people, I can
              imagine you at school never really getting on
              with the other kids, always on the outside,

when the lights go out on the trip you want to go straight to sleep, you get upset with the others for talking, they all bunk off physics, you're the only one that goes in, is that what it was like?

Yeah I can see that. In your uniform. Problem with being a little man, isn't it. You wear short trousers your whole life.

THOMAS   I'm not –

TONY   So are you going to do this or not?

THOMAS   Are you still talking about it?

TONY   I'm standing here with my shirt up waiting.

THOMAS   No. I'm not.

TONY   Unbelievable.

          What a prick.

ISOBEL   Oh look, I have got a mirror. Do you want to borrow it?

THOMAS   No.

ISOBEL   You should.

          You really should.

          Cos you've still got something…

THOMAS   Shut up.

ISOBEL   Shut up. Right. Right.

TONY   Why did your dad call you Thomas? Was he a Christian?

It's not a very nice name. Is it?
Thomas.
Doubting Thomas. Thomas. I suppose you
don't notice it because most people called
Thomas call themselves Tom, which is fine,
which is just a normal name. But you actually
want to be called Thomas. I find that
surprising. Why don't you want to be Tom?

THOMAS   I've always been Thomas.

TONY   At school.

THOMAS   Yeah. I like it. I think it's more…

TONY   More…

THOMAS   I think it's better.

TONY   No no… more…

THOMAS   What?

TONY   More…?

More…?

THOMAS   Distinguished. Than Tom. Yes?

TONY   Distinguished. Huh.

    Distinguished.

THOMAS   Tony's a stupid name.

    Sounds old.

TONY   Old? No.

ISOBEL   I've always liked Tony as a name.

TONY   Thank you. I've always liked Isobel.

ISOBEL	Thank you.
THOMAS	I've always liked Isobel.
ISOBEL	Are you coming on to me?
THOMAS	Why me? He said he liked it too.
ISOBEL	He was coming on to me.
THOMAS	
ISOBEL	So?
THOMAS	Sorry to disappoint I just like the name.
ISOBEL	You know you can get stuff for hair loss?
THOMAS	I'm not losing my hair.
ISOBEL	Oh. Okay. Tony, I was telling Jackie about that thing you were saying. You know.
TONY	With the second series.
ISOBEL	Yeah exactly, she said you were completely right but she had a theory of her own.
TONY	Anyone can have a theory.
ISOBEL	She said to tell you she'll be in The Chequers later to discuss it.
TONY	Good good. You coming?
ISOBEL	Not if you and her want some –
TONY	No no come on, it's not one of those, it's a Thursday, Clangers is there on a Thursday.
ISOBEL	Clangers?
TONY	Yeah yeah.
ISOBEL	I love him! He's so fucking –
	Oh. Sorry. Clangers is this guy. In the pub.

TONY   Yeah, on Thursdays. Why aren't you – You
            don't drink do you? Is that why you've never
            come along?

THOMAS   No one's ever told me.

TONY   What? About Thursdays? Yeah. We must've
            done. Everyone's there on a – You must've
            heard everyone talking about it?
            Isobel haven't you ever told him?

ISOBEL   I assumed you would've.

TONY   Oh.

            Oh no.

            Thomas.

            I'm sorry.

ISOBEL   Well do you want to come tonight?

THOMAS   Why are you asking?

ISOBEL   You might want to drown your sorrows.

THOMAS   Me. Why me? Why not you?

ISOBEL   Because you're not staying.

            Here.

            In your job.

THOMAS   You don't know that.

ISOBEL   Not being funny but –

            Do you want to know what we both know?

            Thomas?

            Do you want to know what we both know?

THOMAS   Only if it's very relevant.

ISOBEL   You tell him. He believes you. He thinks I'm
                a bitch.

TONY   Isobel was in the corridor two days ago, was
                it?

ISOBEL   Yeah

TONY   Yeah on the way back from lunch and she met
                Mr Carter in the corridor, and he said to her, I
                don't want you worrying about this
                procedure, it isn't meant for people like you,
                which kind of means we know she's through.

ISOBEL   Yeah, so then I said well thank you for telling
                me, it's a weight off my shoulders, you know,
                phew! And then I said I'm sorry, I know it's a
                cheeky question but who will I be working
                with? Out of the other two? Can you tell me
                sir or is that top secret? And he said well
                don't tell anyone but it won't be the short
                flabby one.
                As we established earlier, I think that means
                you.

THOMAS   I'm not short.

ISOBEL   You are.

THOMAS   I'm really not.

ISOBEL   You seem it.

THOMAS   He hasn't made a decision. He wouldn't tell
                you. And he wouldn't say that.

ISOBEL   Okay.

                But...

                He did.

THOMAS   He wouldn't.

ISOBEL	I was trying to be nice, and tell you the facts in advance but clearly you don't want to know, so fine
THOMAS	If I believed it, if I really believed what you're saying I wouldn't stick around would I? I'd just go if I thought I'd lost.
ISOBEL	Well yes. Thought you could save face.
THOMAS	Been here two years.
ISOBEL	Doesn't seem to mean a thing these days. I've only been here six months and I'm staying on. How weird is that?
THOMAS	You don't know anything. Just a clever way of getting rid of me.
ISOBEL	Fine.
CARTER	Hello hello.
TONY	Mr Carter.
ISOBEL	Hello.
THOMAS	Hello.
CARTER	Yes. I would say I'm sorry I'm late, but I'm not and you knew didn't you, I let Tony know he told you I was running late I assume he told you all my schedule had slipped.
TONY	We've got a problem sir.
CARTER	What?
TONY	We've had a disagreement.
CARTER	Really.
TONY	Just now while we're waiting.

CARTER	Have you?
THOMAS	It's not important.
CARTER	What?
TONY	Thomas you explain.
THOMAS	No you explain Tony.
TONY	Come on, I think it's better if you lay it out.
CARTER	What's the matter?
THOMAS	They were just playing a stupid game.
CARTER	What game?
THOMAS	Tony lifted up his shirt and Isobel said if I put my face against his chest, will you do the same, and she did, but then I didn't want to so I said no, and then they both had a go at me for going back on the deal, but there wasn't really a deal in the first place.
CARTER	Why do I need to hear this?
THOMAS	Tony brought it up.
CARTER	Tony?
TONY	Um I think there's been some misunderstanding. I was referring to whether we were supposed to bring supporting paperwork today.
CARTER	Then what's he talking about?
TONY	I… sorry. I really don't know.
CARTER	Isobel?
ISOBEL	Sorry… Thomas you're saying he lifted up his shirt and what? I put my face up against it?
THOMAS	It doesn't matter, it's fine. My mistake. I thought we were talking about something else.

CARTER	Well I haven't got this time to lose to be honest with you talking nothing like this I'm running late and the answer to supposed to bring supporting paperwork is of course, that's what I told you Tony. I told you to make that clear to everyone.
TONY	Fine.
THOMAS	I didn't get that message sir.
CARTER	You haven't got any supporting paperwork?
THOMAS	No.
CARTER	Why not?
THOMAS	I didn't know we were supposed to bring it. I assumed this was just a chat.
CARTER	Tony why didn't you tell him?
TONY	I did sir, I told him, and I emailed. I can probably dig it out if you like.
CARTER	No no it's too late now, let's get on with it, you'll just have to manage… what was your name?
THOMAS	Sir?
CARTER	What was your name I've forgotten.
THOMAS	Thomas.
CARTER	Tom, that's right. Tom. So? Come on then, let's have a look at your… thank you.
THOMAS	Do you want me to summarise my figures?
CARTER	What?
THOMAS	Do you want me to tell you what I would've –
CARTER	No no.

These are very good you two.

ISOBEL	Thank you.
TONY	Thank you sir.
CARTER	It's a difficult thing this, you know that, I'm sure you appreciate this, it's always difficult when faced with the need to downsize, when faced with the need to conduct a cull, if I can put it like that, which I think I can, in fact I think that's quite a good word for what we're doing, it's a cull to save the species, by which I mean the rest of us, from extinction, so anyway I've been having these meetings with each team face to face to ask a few questions la la and get the sense, hands on so to speak, as to who should go, you understand, I don't believe in doing this through staring at a graph or just sales figures, or whatever, however impressive they may be, because when it comes down to it you two –
THOMAS	Three.
CARTER	What?
THOMAS	
CARTER	When it comes down to it we're people aren't we, all of us, every single one and we should be treated as human beings.
TONY	Absolutely.
ISOBEL	Yes.
THOMAS	Yes.
CARTER	Not simply product. And it helps me too, I mean already from being here from being face to face in person, I've already drawn some conclusions, and I'm going to be quite honest in this interview I hope you don't mind, but I'll tell you what they are. Isobel uses her looks to compensate for a certain

amount of insecurity, Tony comes from a privileged background I think, from the way he ties his tie, his shoes, from the way he speaks to me, he's used to schoolmasters, he's had a private education, unlike... what was your name?

THOMAS   Thomas.

CARTER   Tom, who is most definitely a comprehensive boy, comp boy done good nothing wrong with that nothing wrong with that at all, but when it's survival of the fittest I'm afraid there's no room for quotas or positive discrimination or worked his way up or anything like that, it's simply about performance, and presentation. Presentation is important. You can quote me on that please do, Tom you have a stain on your jacket.

THOMAS   Oh.

CARTER   You should've worn your best one.

But please, relax, lovely. I might have a little drink, you don't mind do you?

ISOBEL   No

TONY   No.

THOMAS   I'm fine thank you.

CARTER   I'm sorry?

THOMAS   I'm alright for a drink.

CARTER   I wasn't offering.

THOMAS   Oh.

CARTER   I wasn't offering you a drink, I've had a long morning, I can afford to relax a little, but you're fighting for your jobs, I wasn't suggesting you get drunk, is that what you

	need Tom a bit of Dutch courage? You can have one if you like but –
THOMAS	No. I was saying – no. I'm sorry.
CARTER	Alright then. Now.
	You don't work well as a team. I've seen your results. The three of you are fine on your own. But bad as a team. Why?
ISOBEL	Thomas
TONY	Thomas yes.
CARTER	Right.
TONY	We can't work with him. It's him that should go, we both agree on that.
CARTER	It's my decision.
TONY	It's your decision absolutely sir, but we both know Thomas very well, and we thought we'd save you time by giving you the benefit of our experience. Thomas is difficult to work with, he has trouble selling to anyone as his language and presentational skills are non-existent, he often comes into work with dandruff and with breath that smells and these things not only put off clients but are clearly distracting him from the task in hand.
ISOBEL	I've also found sir that he has issues with women, I think since his relationship finished six months ago, he's developed a real resentment towards us. He often uses sexist language, and I believe that far from having a professional relationship with me he fantasises about something sexual a lot of the time and knowing this makes me feel distinctly uncomfortable in his presence.
CARTER	Are you uncomfortable now?

ISOBEL	Distinctly sir yes.
THOMAS	Can I answer all of that sir?
CARTER	When we've finished I think you should. So you believe he's simply a bad apple?
TONY	An average of ten per cent of employees underperform, and if it wasn't for current employment legislation, would be replaced immediately. I think one of the few benefits of this economic crisis and consequent redundancies is to clear some of the chaff away and I do believe he is prime chaff, yes. I see no reason for continuing to employ him if you have to reduce the staff by one third, which you do. I think when you've got the three of us here in front of you sir you would have no difficulty making the correct decision. I think by any criteria you would remove the right person.
CARTER	You two seem to have this sewn up.
ISOBEL	This isn't bias sir, this is simply about business, about sales figures.
THOMAS	It's bullying.
TONY	You see. That's exactly what we're talking about. He's said one thing in all of this and it's become personal straight away when nothing we were saying was personal at all.
CARTER	Bullying?
THOMAS	Yes, they just don't like me, this is nothing to do with business.
CARTER	They say they don't get on with you.
THOMAS	That's not my fault.

CARTER	No?
THOMAS	No, they have some thing going on between the two of them and it leaves me out, I think I've been unlucky to be put with them maybe they have a relationship or something I don't know I'm not part of their clique but there's obviously something going on which means all that they've said, their ability to get on with me, is biased and the work of the team is compromised by their personal feelings towards me. I am here to do a job, I'm not here to make friends, but for whatever reason they feel compelled to torment me
CARTER	Torment –
THOMAS	And I've had enough I want to make an official complaint of harassment and bullying –
CARTER	You want to make an official complaint?
THOMAS	Yes absolutely – I can put up with a certain amount but if it's going to get to this, if it's actually going to affect the outcome of something like this –
CARTER	You're making me feel like a schoolteacher Tom.
THOMAS	No. Sir.
CARTER	A babysitter. Like I have to protect you.
THOMAS	No, that's not –
CARTER	You're an adult.
THOMAS	I know.
CARTER	Stand up for yourself.
THOMAS	It's not as simple as that.
TONY	You see sir?

ISOBEL	You see?
THOMAS	I have stood up for myself but –
CARTER	It always has been as simple as that, for me, always worked in my experience, standing up for myself, I never found myself intimidated or put off my work by colleagues I was single-minded.
THOMAS	Well that's you sir, and I'm me, and we're different, and I do try, I'm not bad at my job, I just don't go around sticking knives in people's backs.
CARTER	You think that's what they're doing?
THOMAS	I think so yes, I think this is all basically fun for them, they want to hurt me.
CARTER	Okay okay, look you do realise Tom you're not doing yourself any favours using emotive language like that. Talking about knives and and backs or whatever. They don't look to me as if they are out to hurt you, it looks to me like they are professionals who don't waste time and that maybe you can't keep up with them.
THOMAS	I can. I can keep up, but not when I'm being attacked every –
CARTER	No. No.
THOMAS	Every day when I sit there on the train into work every single day just going over and over, worrying about what's going to happen to me when I come into work whether, I'll overhear them saying something, or whether they'll –
CARTER	Tom
THOMAS	Whether they'll decide to give me the right bits of information, he didn't tell me about the file today

CARTER	Tom
THOMAS	I could've prepared the figures if he'd told me but he, they deliberately left me pissing in the fucking –
CARTER	Tom
THOMAS	Sorry.
CARTER	Alright.

You don't work as a team, that's clear.

We don't need to give this any more time.

The two of you are outstanding.

Tom, well, obviously for whatever reason it's not working out for you here, so we're going to let you go. We'll give you official notice on this and so forth, but we're operating a policy that you can leave as soon as you like, and in your case perhaps that's best, if you speak to human resources they'll give you the details of the package, but sooner the better I think, yes? I'm sorry this had to happen but there we are. It sounds like we'll all be actually happier in this particular case.

ISOBEL	I think so.
TONY	Yes.
THOMAS	I won't get another job.
CARTER	I'm sorry?
THOMAS	The way things are at the moment. I won't find something else. I won't be happier. I want to stay here.

CARTER	Doesn't sound like it.
THOMAS	This is unfair.
CARTER	I'm sorry?
THOMAS	I can appeal.
CARTER	You can.
THOMAS	Right.
CARTER	But if you win, and stay, I'll make your life a nightmare because I don't like to be told what I can and can't do. And if you lose, it goes on your record, it affects your reference.
	So yes. You can. Appeal.
	If you want.
	Or you can just go, quietly.
THOMAS	
CARTER	
THOMAS	
CARTER	Right.
	See you two later.
TONY	Short
THOMAS	Shut up.
TONY	I meant the meeting, the *meeting* was short, jesus.
ISOBEL	I thought he'd ask a lot more questions.
TONY	Me too.
ISOBEL	But I suppose the decision must've just been really easy.

TONY   Yeah, really obvious.

ISOBEL   Really clear that one of us wasn't up to muster.

                Sorry Thomas.

TONY   Sorry mate.

ISOBEL   Not your day really is it?

TONY   When is your day?
                Perhaps you've had your day already.

THOMAS   Fuck off.

TONY   Oooo.

ISOBEL   Shame.

TONY   Yeah.

ISOBEL   You'd hope for a bit of grace or something.

TONY   You'd hope for dignity.

                After all this time, working together, as
                colleagues, you'd hope actually, that he'd
                understand – that all's fair when it comes
                down to it. That it's nothing personal, it's just
                the bottom line. You'd hope he wouldn't hold
                it against us, and that in fact, maybe, after all
                this time, we'd have a little hug. Like they do
                on *The Apprentice*, when one of them's been
                kicked out. They have a little hug sometimes.
                Don't they?

                Shall we do that?

                Thomas?

                Come on. Let's have a little hug.

                Come on.

                Come here.

THOMAS   Fuck off.

TONY   Come on.

                 You want to.

                 You do.

                 There. That's better.

                 Isn't it?

                 There.

                 Okay then.

                 I'm going to head, got some paperwork to be
                 done this afternoon, you alright if I leave you
                 to…?

ISOBEL   Yeah, you go on, I'm quite able to –

TONY   Mop up. Good. See you Thomas, hope you
                 find something soon, I'm sure… I'm sure you
                 will… find something… something… in the
                 end… I'm sure… even you… will find
                 something… I mean there are still some jobs
                 that no one wants to do… so you could get
                 one of those… if you need to…

                 Thomas.

                 You've still got it.

THOMAS   Right.

TONY   I mean it.

THOMAS   Yeah thanks. I know.

TONY   Just there. On the right.

                 You've still got something on your… never
                 mind.

ISOBEL   I feel really sorry for you.

THOMAS   It's alright you can go.

ISOBEL   – *really* sorry. I do. I promise. I do. I'm
            feeling sorrow. Right now.

            You have a kid don't you?

            You do.

            I know you do.

            So.

            So you don't need to hide it.

            You have a kid.

THOMAS   Yeah.

ISOBEL   Yeah. Tough. What's its name?

            Is it Harry?

            It is Harry.

            I know it is.

            You know how I know this?

            It's because once when we left work, I was
            walking behind you and you walked all the
            way down the road, and I could see you in
            front of me, and I saw you meet this woman
            in a coffee shop it wasn't a nice coffee shop I
            was surprised you went into it, it was a
            Starbucks or something not even a good one
            a shit Starbucks, a Shitbucks, and I watched
            you meet this woman and she had a little
            toddling little thing, and I waited and I saw

you go to the loo, and then I ran in and said
oh I was hoping to catch you and I pretended
I was in a hurry, and I had a little chat with
Marion, is that her name your ex and she
told me about Harry, and I said I was a
colleague and you were taking ages in the
toilet actually we talked about it we didn't
know what you were up to in there, but it
meant we had a good talk about you, and in
the end when you still didn't come out I said
I needed to dash and I'd catch you tomorrow
instead, but that conversation with her gave
me quite a lot of crucial information.

Which I've always known when you've tried
to hide things or lie or whatever, I've always
known about your life things that you don't
know I know. I know you have to pay
Marion that certain amount every month and
when she hears that you're out of work her
low estimation of you will drop even further
it will I promise she won't be surprised that's
the really tragic thing, she won't be like oh
my God you lost your job! Oh my God!
She'll be like, yeah of course he lost his job
fucking retard good thing I got out while I
could, better not let him see Harry too much
don't want Harry to grow up in the distorted
disabled image of his fucking drip drip of a
father.

I expect that's what she'll think.

It's tough isn't it, life.

Is it a lot more difficult than you imagined it
would be?

I mean I'm sure you thought it was difficult
but that through sheer hard work, and practice
and training and long hours and inspiration

and in your case perspiration you would come through and in the end, succeed, because you thought that despite everything, it was, in this country at least, a meritocracy and that fair play and honest, transparent behaviour at work would be rewarded in the end. That bad people like me would fall at the wayside and good people like you would triumph.

That's what you thought isn't it?

Oops.

THOMAS	Don't you feel any guilt?
ISOBEL	Guilt? No. Sorrow? Yes. Guilt…?
THOMAS	Don't you feel any –
ISOBEL	No.
THOMAS	You don't feel –
ISOBEL	No.

I don't feel anything like that because I think I know in my heart that if it wasn't me there would be someone else doing this to you, I think I know in the deepest bit of my heart that actually you bring all of this on yourself I don't behave like this to most people I just let most people get on with their lives or I share a joke or whatever but for some reason with you I feel the need to bring you down I think it might be an evolved thing in a society in a culture, that if we see someone who's going to bring down the whole tribe or whatever someone who's really going to fuck up the rest of us because they're stupid or slow or weak or thin or short or or ugly or has dandruff or something you have the desire somewhere deep within you to take them down first to get rid of them and strengthen the tribe that's all I'm doing with this that's why I'm inexplicably drawn to you all the time poking and poking and poking and poking and poking and poking and poking and being fucking awful to you and you're right we are both of us Tony and me we're really horrible to you, you're not imagining it, it was real, but that's why, because I think it's instinct, and I think it goes on all the time I think it's actually everywhere I think it's actually how things are supposed to be.

I also don't think you'll see much of your son as he grows up because you're right what you said to Carter you won't get another job easily I expect this one was a stretch really when you got it so you know the next one won't come easy and you're not the kind of guy to have lots of friends are you? So you'll probably go home tonight in a minute on your own, call your mum or your best friend and tell them what's happened and they'll be a bit sympathetic but again they won't be surprised and really they'll feel annoyed that now this is on their plate as well, my idiot son who can't keep his job, my best mate, who I made friends with at school now he's homeless, face down in the –

Woah woah, that was lashing out. Hey you nearly hit me physically physical violence against a woman, lucky I do my self-defence classes, you could've hurt me if I wasn't lithe and brilliant.

THOMAS   Fuck off.

ISOBEL   Have another go, try and hit me again.

                No, missed. Again.

                Missed.

                I'm like a cat. I prance, I jump, I'm like a
                Soviet gymnast, I'm really perfect physically
                and mentally, you ever noticed that, people
                with good clear physically fit bodies tend to
                have the minds to match. Your brain is a bit
                weedy, and short.

                Missed again.

                Again!

                And again!

                Tired yet?

THOMAS   Leave me alone.

ISOBEL   One last go.

                Go on.

                Okay.

                Okay.

                Ooo!

                Ow.

                Careful.

                Owch. Are you alright?

Eek.

Okay. Um…

Look I'm just going to leave you here, alright, but… before I do.

Before I do.

There.

We clubbed together this morning in the office and got you this. It's a single malt. We had a feeling it would be you who'd be going and we thought we'd save time… oh.

But you don't drink, do you?

Do you want it anyway?

Because you might want to start?

When you wake up.

A drink might be just the thing.

Okay?

Thomas?

Yes?

Right.

We didn't bother with a card. Didn't have much to say. Most of them couldn't remember who you were… so…

I'll just leave the whisky here.

Good luck.

End.

A Nick Hern Book

Bull first published in Great Britain in 2013 as a paperback original by Nick Hern Books Limited, The Glasshouse, 49a Goldhawk Road, London W12 8QP, in association with Sheffield Theatres

Reprinted in this revised edition in 2015, in association with the Young Vic, London

Cover image: courtesy of Muse Design

Designed and typeset by Nick Hern Books, London
Printed in Great Britain by CPI Group (UK) Ltd

A CIP catalogue record for this book is available from the British Library

ISBN 978 1 84842 466 1